Give Me This Mountain

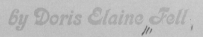

by Doris Elaine Fell

Scripture quotations in this volume are from King James.

Illustrations: Alice Paschal

Published by:
WYCLIFFE BIBLE TRANSLATORS, INC.
Huntington Beach, California

Library of Congress Catalog Card Number: 74-28538

Design: Saralee Debley and Hyatt Moore
Cover photo: Earl Adams

TABLE OF HAPPENINGS

Preface

Give Me This Mountain is a collection of "happenings" at Jungle Camp in Chiapas, Mexico. Since they were written as minute meditations in 1959, they have been a source of blessing to numerous campers and staff alike.

Although some of the "happenings" have altered through the years, the entire series is Jungle Camp. All through *Give Me This Mountain* you will see God's hand at work as was the author's intention.

Doris Elaine "Till" Fell attended J.C. Session I, 1959, as a camper. Since that time she served with Wycliffe in the Philippines and Guatemala. She has also served on the SIL staff at the Summer Institute of Linguistics and as an Editorial Assistant for *Translation* magazine.

Arrival

We left to the tune of Jingle Bells
                    and Noel
                    and Silent Night.
          just before the snow storm of January.

We left with the taste of turkey still in our mouth
                              and families
                              and unwrapped presents
             both by the lighted Christmas tree.

Some goodbyes were more tearful
          because we went in opposition;

Some were with greater assurance
          because of prayerful backing.

          YET NO GOODBYE IS EASY.

          It was good to be on the way
                    in groups of over-packed cars,
                    by planes in spite of strikes,
                    alone by Greyhound.

     How could we tell our families
                    and friends
                    and churches
               that we were called?

     We were not the heroes
                    nor idiots
                    nor martyrs
               they claimed us to be.

We were simply believers in the Lord Jesus.
We were the foolish and weak and base and
despised of I Corinthians.
We were the ones whose hearts yearned within
us to please Him.

Perhaps we were yet a little frightened
a little hesitant
about Jungle Camp.

But we went
with our duffle bag of equipment supplied.
with our transportation fund in hand.
with our every need met.

rejoicing in His provision.
rejoicing in the growth of those we loved.
rejoicing in His working in our lives.

Expectantly we went —

*"And Asa cried unto the Lord his God, and said, Lord, it is
nothing with Thee to help, whether with many, or with them that have
no power: help us, oh Lord our God: For we rest on Thee, and in Thy
name we go . . ."*

Village Visitation

We could say, "Hello"
             "Goodbye"
              and "What is this?"

(A rather limited vocabulary for village visitation.)

Fortunately our first visits were to believers. And though they may have thought us rather strange, they accepted us and would respond to our ever persistent question — "What is this?"

Our vocabulary increased somewhat.
And so did our visits.

We seemed more ridiculous in our arrival.
And the village assignments were further away.

We began to see some of what we will see in our own field appointments:

— beautiful countryside:
mountain grandeur
rippling rivers
fabulous sunsets
gigantic trees
unusual flowers.

BUT THIS WAS GOD'S CREATION!

— small hidden villages:
isolated people
thatched roofs
smoke-filled huts
pigs running freely
unusual sights.

BUT THIS WAS MAN'S CREATION!

We could turn back
                    to home
                    and good paying jobs
                    and conveniences.

                              away from loneliness,
                              away from long, muddy trails,
                              away from responsibility.

"How then shall they call on Him in whom they have not believed?
And how shall they believe in Him of whom they have not heard?
And how shall they hear without a preacher?
And how shall they preach, except they be sent? As it is written,
How beautiful are the feet of them that preach the Gospel of peace,
                              and bring glad tidings of good things."

There are many villages.
     There are so many, many people.
          There are so many different languages.

Oh, that they might recognize
                              God's beauty.
                              God's Son.
                              God's love.

Then saith He unto His people,

     The villages truly are plenteous

        but the translators are few;

          Pray ye therefore the Lord of the villages,

             that He will send forth translators into these villages.

Our First Overnight

The experienced and the inexperienced gathered.
They were easily distinguished!

      The light packs.
           The over-weighted duffles.

      The sharpened machetes.
           The dull-edged ones.

      The hiking boots.
           The sport shoes.

    The distance was short (for some).
    The task rather difficult (for others).
Jungle hammocks were not easily hung
                the first time . . .
                nor the second . . .

    Dusk and darkness fell;
          and later so did some of the hammocks.

Is this missionary training?
Is this soul-winning?
      It is preparation,
      And God would have us prepared
           — for every situation.

We may hang our hammocks someday
          in a pioneer situation
          on a trail to someone in need . . .
                  of Christ.

We needed that night in the jungle

    alone
    alone in a hammock
    alone in the presence of God.

We needed to hear Him call again
    and to cry out, "Here am I . . ."

AND DAVID?
      WHEN HE WAS AFRAID?

"What time I am afraid, I will trust in Thee . . . Thou tellest my wanderings; put Thou my tears into Thy bottle; are they not in Thy book? When I cry unto Thee, then shall mine enemies turn back; this I know; for God is for me . . . In God have I put my trust: I will not be afraid what man can do unto me. THY VOWS ARE UPON ME, O GOD: I will render praises unto Thee."

AND I, TOO, WEPT —

    "Thy vows are upon me, O God."

Even Swimming

"I can't — I'm scared."
　　　　a drippy mess —
　　　　of wet green skirt,
　　　　red swim hat,
　　　　water-logged sneakers
　　　　and defiance.

　　　　And what is the basis of this disobedience?
　　　　And whom do you disobey?

"I'm scared," says
　　　　　　　the missionary recruit
　　　　　　　and the mission board
　　　　　　　and the weary missionary.

"I'm scared,"
　　　　the translator cries.

　　　　Of what?
　　　　Of whom?

　　　　"I'm scared."
　　　　　　　— is that the time to quit?
　　　　　　　or to look up?

　　　It is time to trust the Sufficient One
　　　　　　　and to prove Him.
　　　We find His tower of strength.
　　　We find our sufficiency in Him . . .

　　　　　　for applying to a Board.
　　　　　　in prayerfully considering candidates.
　　　　　　for difficulties on the field.
　　　　　　in translating the Word.

AND EVEN IN SWIMMING!

The "I CAN'T" becomes an "I CAN"

> *"I can . . .*
> I can *do all things . . .*
> I can do all things *through Christ . . .*
> I can do all things through Christ
>   *which strengtheneth me!"*

Building Projects

A project of our very own choosing.

Blueprints were very hastily prepared and shown to our instructor. Poles were grabbed and spots selected. The sounds of saws, hammers, and "I can't" voices could be heard.

The days sped by,
        And the weeks,
                And the time.

Sixteen poles — then twenty-two — then twenty-four.

There were many rough edges and hastily made holes. Uneven measurements. Care should have been given; but suddenly we were called away.

The projects were in various stages of construction. Some were completed and useful. Some broke with use. One or two never went beyond their original beginning. Occasionally a builder could be seen attempting to finish . . . but always busied by other activities. Some which started out to be one thing became another. Few ever became the replica of the blueprints.

And our lives. What of them? What of the sudden call which will one day come to us?

As builders where do we stand? Are we constructing as God intended us to do? Are we all that He has planned? Have we "short-cutted" here and there? Are we smoothed and refined? Are we measured well — and with care?

Are we building as God intended us to build?

As we are patterned and built do we resemble
the original blueprint?

*"For which of you, intending to build a tower, sitteth not
down first, and counteth the cost, whether he have sufficient
to finish it?*

*Lest haply, after he hath laid the foundation, and is not able
to finish it, all that behold it begin to mock him,*

Saying, this man began to build, and was not able to finish."

Our Clinic Hour

"Mach'a ya ya'iy chamel?"
    (Who is sick?)
"Bin ora jajch achamel?"
    (When did your sickness start?)

They came to us — inexperienced missionaries — with our
limited language experience — into the clinic with its strange smells
and responsibilities . . . and with their needs!

In need, physically:
                colds
                anemia
                malnutrition
                malaria
                injured limbs
                infections.

        and we gave them:
                    pills
                    injections
                    medicines.

In need, materially:
                bare feet
                some thinly clad
                the men with hats and sandals.

        and we pity them:
                    in our pride
                    and our material riches
                    our unrecognized abundance.

They came

    In need, spiritually:

                they do not know it.
                and sometimes
                we wonder
                do we know it ourselves.

      and we pity them:

                but why?
                for which need?
                and how — in love?

They came by ones, by twos,
                in groups,
                by multitudes.

    — with their needs!!!

"And Jesus went about all the cities and villages, teaching in their synagogues, and preaching the Gospel of the Kingdom, and healing every sickness and every disease among the people, BUT when He saw the multitudes, He was moved . . ."

    — with pity?   — NO!

"with compassion on them because they fainted, and were scattered abroad as sheep having no shepherd."

The Baer Battle

This was the first divided hike
    — and the first long one.
We had a destination
    — but mostly a name to us.

Out through the camp gate we trudged
    an oddly dressed lot
        with pack racks and morrales
            and over-weighted web belts.

It seemed more like fun than a battle.

    (We had been training and hiking.
        We had been preparing.
    But battles are strange
        and we come upon them unknowingly
        not realizing the greatness of the conflict.)

We marched out through the gate
    — a crooked line of eager trainees.
Just over the hillside the clouds came
    — and the drops began to fall.
By the time we made camp that night
    signs of defeat began to possess us.
We were wet and cold and miserable.
    — we were weary from walking.

    The jungle hammocks did not keep out the rain . . .

The sky was starless — and hearts were
cold.
Daylight came and we broke camp
                              and moved out.
                    into the unknown . . .
                      into the jungle trail . . .
                          into the wet and cold and rain.

(And our Captain said, "This is the
day which the Lord hath made; we will
rejoice and be glad in it.")

                              up the mountain side . . . slipping
and tumbling blindly and angrily through ankle-deep mud.
Struggling against the elements
          and self
          and the One who was leading
          and mules
          and the day "which the Lord had made".

                    Our packs were heavy . . .
                    Our clothing was wet . . .
                    Our spirits were dampened.

The guns we carried for hunting were ever ready for use. But the armor
was rusty. The battle was long and tiring. Reaching the top of Baer
Hill was only to reach it in defeat.

*And JEHOSHAPHAT and all JUDAH gathered themselves
together to ask the help of the Lord. "For we have no might against
this great company that cometh against us; neither know we what to do:
but our eyes are upon Thee . . . Be not afraid nor dismayed by reason
of this great multitude; for the battle is not yours, but God's."*

As we tumbled into our ever wet hammocks that night we had to
look up and in tears admit that our eyes had not been upon Thee.

And when the battle was over
And the victory was won,
We hiked back over the trails;
We marched back into camp,
a mud-caked, wiser group.

And told those who awaited us warmly

of the days "which the Lord had made,"
of protection against snakes,
of tasty fudge,
of the faithfulness of the Baers,
of the Lacandons who need the Saviour,
of the sun-filled Sunday,
of the trail to the village of Lacandon,
of the fellowship with believers there.

of temperaments subdued.
of hearts convicted.
of needs met.

We told them of our battle and of our victory and joyfully said,

— "THE BATTLE WAS NOT OURS BUT HIS."

The Canoe Trip

My memories of the canoe trip are sweet.
   "My meditation of Him shall be sweet."

Four canoes.
   Fourteen people.
      A beautiful day.

               up river
               gliding, splashing
               past the beautiful countryside;

               with the warmth of the sun,
                  the reflection of the water,
                    and the rhythm of motion.

It was so refreshing to be at peace,
and though wet, to be clean.

(The mud-caked boots of the Baer trip were in contrast.)

Hammocks were hung.
   Fishing attempted.
      Food devoured.

Some swam (bathed).
   Some retired (early).
      Some sat by the glowing fireside.

Each was free to meditate.
And truly "meditation of Him was sweet."

Morning brought more sunlight,
    A hike beside the turbulent waters of the canyon
        And much rejoicing in His creation.

The splash and the wetness . . .
    The gliding and tipping of canoes . . .
      The tour through the rapids . . .
        The gathering of orchids . . .
          The time out for swimming . . .
        The joy of return.

All are sweet memories.

My memories of the canoe trip became so sweet
    that the bitterness of El Capulin was gone.

"How sweet are Thy Words unto my taste!
Yea sweeter than honey to my mouth."
    (and bitterness goes)

    "My meditation of Him shall be sweet:
      — I will be glad in the Lord."

Agua Escondida

Agua Escondida, the Hidden Water!

    It sounded like a place of beauty.
      A Shangri-la.
        A place to be desired.
          Perhaps faintly like the city of God.

For "There is a river, the streams whereof shall make glad the city of
God . . . God is in the midst of her."

    We have known that we would be going there.
    We have anticipated the going.
    We have been preparing for it.

    It is a place of history
      but of past history.
    We will see the Mayan temple — the ruins —
      of a once triumphant era.
    And we will see decay.

    We will take little with us
      — only part of our things.
    We have set aside food for that time
      not only for six days
      but with the possibility
      of seven
      or eight.
    We are not sure when we will leave there.

Is our vision limited to Agua Escondida, to the Mayan ruins?
Or are we looking "for a city which hath foundations whose builder
and maker is God?"

We have known that we would be going there.
We have anticipated the going.
We have been preparing for it.

It was in the ages past
and ever eternal.
We will see the throne of God — and see —
The True, Triumphant King
And we shall live.

We will take nothing with us
— "nothing in our hands to bring."
We have set aside nothing here
for all treasures are there.
And we will be staying
forever
and ever.

Agua Escondida —

The staff has said to be ready early.

AND GOD?

has said that *"Heaven and earth shall pass away . . . But
of that day and that hour knoweth no man, no not the
angels which are in heaven, neither the Son, but the
Father. Take ye heed, watch and pray; for ye know
not when the time is."*

*"Therefore be ye also ready: For in such an hour as ye think not the
Son of Man cometh!"*

In Appreciation

From all the S.I.L.s — from Boston and Canada —
　　From different schools and varied walks of life —
And each one of us by a miracle of Grace —
　　By plane — by car — by bus — by tow chain
　　We came into Mexico.

We came with expectations high — with over-stuffed
duffle bags —
　　With various mishaps.
Yet with the assurance of His leading
　　we reached the airstrip at Ixtapa!
Flight reactions varied but the first glimpse of J.C.
　　was one and the same — aerial and unique in its setting.

　　As it came closer to us
　　　　and we to it — we felt the ground touch us —
　　　　and before our exit, we heard the welcome of
　　　　staff and kiddies and Sheppie, the dog.

　　We sensed the warmth of welcome and we were at home!
　　We were grateful for this.

Six weeks' rush of activities and learning
　　with suddenness is gone.
　　We are almost anxious to be gone . . .
　　　　to advance to Advance Base . . .
　　　　to taste of village living . . .
　　　　to be within reach of tribal assignments . . .
　　　　to be in haste to the place of His choice for us.

There will be some last minute duffle stuffing.
    Some sleepy-eyed packers.
    And as you send us over the trail
    and see us disappear over the hillside
    there will be no rest at all for you.
        New flights in — new campers —
        another warm welcome for you to extend.

We wonder what your remembrance of us will be.
    Breaches of discipline?
        Frustrations?
            Kitchen gripes?
          Hard heads?
              Mud-caked hikers?
                  Tipped canoes?

We earnestly feel that we are taking everything with us.
We have left a few things:

    Some kindling poles in the carpentry shop.
    Screws and bolts by the motors we put together.
    A number of left-overs in the refrig
    and Robert Morrison in the library.

The rest we take with us.
We are grateful for these
delightful recollections —
these happy memories
of Jungle Camp!

        Our little thatched-roof huts.
        Original bread boards
        and spoons and potty seats . . .
            and candle holders — never seen before
                — and most likely —
            never to be seen again.

Phrases of Tzeltal and methods of approach — BUT MORE . . .
A remembrance of our final Tzeltal class and its exhortation to
faithfulness and fruitfulness.

A family-like remembrance of our devotions and Bible-shared
Sundays.

An appreciation for the entire staff in their patience in dealing
with us and in instructing us. An appreciation for their willingness
to share in our learning.

And a thankfulness for their obvious understanding and prayer-
fulness as we in our training have seen a fresh glimpse of the One
"who had no rights of his own."

We know as campers come and go, we may be but names and
faces to you. We may become mingled in the sea of remembrances
which Jungle Camp affords for you.

As for us, J.C. will ever be a part of preparation; and as for us in
our reflections, we will thank *"our God upon every remembrance
of you."*

To Advance Base

We were advancing!
New recruits were coming
and we were advancing:

to Advance Base
ten hours away.

It is not easy to hike
            when the day is hot.
            the traveler weary.
            and the shoes borrowed.

It is harder at noon
            with the sun beating down.
            when the blisters start rubbing.
            and the ticks start crawling.
            (and the babies cry).

    The training
        The experiences
            The lectures
                — of Main Base

            were only a taste of that which
            awaited us. We would be putting
            these into practical usefulness.

Hiking clothes hardly seem the outfit of a soldier.
The crooked line of recruits, rounding the trail,
            hardly seemed a soldier's march
Yet we belonged to an Army — and to a Captain.

And every thought of Advance Base,
      Every expectation, every hesitation,
            Everything that awaited us
                  bore the same exhortation . . .

            "Thou therefore endure hardness, as a
            good soldier of Jesus Christ . . . that (you)
            may please Him who hath chosen (you) *to*
            be a soldier."

Champas in the Making

"This will perhaps be the most trying week of your whole life."

Well thanks — !
Must you make everything so difficult?
If I were on my own field — I'd have a
native build my home.

WOULD YOU? . . . so went my thoughts.

Seven days to make something out of nothing.
Seven days before classes would begin.

In the meantime —

We looked at our uncleared jungle area.
By champa-mates we began to clear away the brush.
(Machetes dull with much hacking.)
Hours later we found that we had cleared by a dead tree.
(And we began again.)

Our duffles of clothing were left on the ground.
   — dressing meant a search.
Our nights were spent in hammocks.
   — our days at work.

And there was no order —
nor neatness.
And we hated the mess.

Support trees and ridge poles.
Cane leaves and cane poles.
Hour after hour of gathering material for the
champa.

AND EVER IT SEEMED —

the appearance of a staff member.

"More canc.
More poles . . ."

In the meantime —

out-door cooking.
smoke and seldom fire.
and missed meals.

When the framework was up,
we began the roof of cane leaves.
One, two, three rows.

AND EVER IT SEEMED —

the appearance of a staff member.

"More cane.
More rows . . ."

In the meantime —

We hacked a trail toward the Center,
working hard and long,
but never meeting;
only to find that native helpers
would soon clear a path for us instead.

We lost track by days
(but days later) we had our roof on
and we began to build the furniture.
The beds were first, end to end.
And happily that night we did not sway
but rested comfortably
upon a bed of cane poles (varied sizes)
beneath our mosquito nets.

In the meantime —

The table (the height of a soda fountain).
And a bench (which lasted a couple of weeks).
And then the sturdy stove.

Its frame was up;
more cane poles were cut.

AND EVER IT SEEMED —
                              the appearance of a staff member.

                              "Is that your stove?
                              Well, hurry.
                              You must get it done."

And finally
the kitchen work table,
the clothes' shelf,
and everything in order.

It hardly seemed possible.
   The once uncleared jungle area — cleared!
   A champa of our very own up!
   What wonders we had wrought "by our own hands."
   A champa of our very own — the "Tiltin' Hilton."

We began to reflect on days just past.
Had there been no battle —
        there would have been no triumph!

NO. This was not a champa "of our very own made by our own hands."

It had been as He had enabled us —
        our tired aching bodies.
It had been in His strength —
        for the struggles had been numerous.
It had been His sufficiency —
        for we were insufficient in ourselves.

*"For every house is builded by some man, but He that built all
things is God."*

This had been a very different week of learning Jesus Christ. We looked
at our "Tiltin' Hilton" with an overwhelming love. We could say with
Paul, *"Now thanks be unto God, which always causeth us to triumph in
Christ, and maketh manifest the savour of His knowledge by us in
EVERY PLACE!"* ("For we are unto God a sweet savour of Christ.")

Fire Frustrations

Fire! Food! and frustrations! The time consuming element of the stomach-minded individual.

Hunger
  Anger
    Resentment
      Complaint
        Rebellion
          . . . against circumstances.

Match after match!
  Hour after hour!
    Day after day!

The sin of hunger.
  The sin of anger.
    The sin of resentment.
      The sin of complaint.
        The sin of rebellion
          . . . against God.

One gathers the fire tinder and passes a fellow camper sitting on the bench quietly reading the Word.

One fans the fire and hears neighboring champa-ites sing a song of praise.

It indicates an early breakfast
        or lunch
          or supper
            and the needful time
              of praising Him.

And one fans the fire harder.

The smoke grows thicker. The tears flow more from smoke's irritation than ever before. More wood is chipped — hopefully — all of the time with an awareness that another even then is kneeling in prayer perhaps a champa away.

Time for reading after the hunger.
Time to sing after the hunger.
Time to pray after the hunger.

CONVICTION!

The sin of hunger grows.
The sin of anger increases.
The sin of resentment mushrooms.
The sin of complaint continues.
The sin of rebellion deepens.

"Now it came to pass, as they went, that He (Jesus) *entered into a certain village: and a certain woman named Martha received Him into her house.*

And she had a sister called Mary, which also sat at Jesus' feet, and heard His Word.

But Martha was cumbered about much serving and came to Him, and said, Lord, dost Thou not care that my sister hath left me to serve alone? Bid her therefore that she help me.

And Jesus answered and said unto her, Martha, Martha, thou art careful and troubled about many things:

BUT ONE THING IS NEEDFUL: and Mary hath chosen that good part, which shall not be taken away from her."

Survival Hike

Survival hike for the fellows was over. The girls became more cautious
and more amusing in appearance. The weather was warm but class
found the girls with jackets,

>   sweaters,
>   flannel shirts,
>   sweat shirts.

The additional bulkiness of appearance was suggestive of jeans (rolled
up); canteens, machetes, first aid kits, flash lights — all attached to
web belts — proved strange equipment for lecture class.

BUT THE GIRLS WERE PREPARED!

The important announcement came on a Wednesday, "Girls, report to
the dock in fifteen minutes."

There was a mad scramble to champas to dispose of skirts and to grab
a last minute banana.

>   A half-hour down river by motored-canoe.
>   Another half-hour into tick infested jungle.
>   WE WERE LOST!

Individual emergency shelters — fifty yards apart.
   Individual fires — to keep us warm.
      Individual cane-poled beds — above the ground.

>   Eight shells — for hunting food.
>   Fishing lines — to utilize.
>   A compass — for direction.

Have you ever spent a night alone
                    (in the jungle?)
Have you ever hunted food
                    (from necessity?)
Have you ever been lost
                    (really lost?)

Men are lost without Jesus Christ.
Men have been lost — martyred — in search of these.

And was ours but a game?

The dreaded survival hike became a blessed time.
    Panic
        Hunger
            Cold
                Ticks
                    Dangers
                        The aloneness
are not expected sources of blessing.
But that night
                    (though little in physical rest)
                was rest in HIM.

For I did
        "Lift up mine eyes unto the hills" (which surrounded me),
from whence my help came. *"My help cometh from the Lord, which
made heaven and earth. He will not suffer thy foot to be moved. He
that keepeth thee will not slumber . . . The Lord is thy keeper: the
Lord is thy shade upon thy right hand. The sun shall not smite thee
by day"* (and we knew safety our second day out, and our third),
"Nor the moon by night" (a second night in His keeping).

"The Lord shall preserve thee from all evil" (from all panic, hunger, cold, ticks, dangers, and the aloneness).

"He shall preserve thy soul" (in nearness to Him).

"The Lord shall preserve thy going out and thy coming in from this time forth, and even for evermore."

In His Keeping

"Thou art mine."
>   (when something belongs to us we tend to
>   love it, guard it, protect it and keep it with
>   care.)

"Thou art mine."
>   (the Lord says to each one of us.)

>   He loves us — "with an everlasting love."
>   He guards us — "He . . . will not slumber."
>   He protects us — "God is our refuge and strength."
>   He keeps us — "The Lord is thy keeper."

"Thou art mine."
>   We have truly experienced His protection,
>   His presence.

>   On the highway to Mexico:
>>   KEPT FROM ALL DANGERS:
>>>   from accident ourselves.
>>>   though ignorant of the law.
>>>   against complications in offering help.
>>>   in thumbing into Mexico City.

>   In training as missionary recruits:
>>   KEPT BY HIS POWER:
>>>   from turning back.
>>>   from quitting.
>>>   from failure.
>>>>   ("I have prayed for thee
>>>>   that thy faith fail not.")
>>>   from self-will and pride.

Through weeks of preparation:
        KEPT FROM ALL HARM:
                from poisonous snakes (five
                        known occasions).
                from riding accidents (when
                        thrown from mules).
                from river dangers (in canoes
                        and swimming).
                from severe burns (with boiled
                        water).
                from machetes and carelessness
                        (when lost on the trail)!

    By days of His leading:
        KEPT IN HIS WORD:
                for day by day guidance
                and daily we ask
                for love that was lacking
                and strength for the task.

"Thou art mine."
        Oh, blessed thought —

                                in the jungle.
                                in training.
                                in the tribe.

"Thou art mine . . .
        When thou passest through the waters, I will be with thee;
and through the rivers, they shall not overflow thee: when thou
walkest through the fire, thou shalt not be burned; neither shall the
flame kindle upon thee. For I am the Lord thy God, the Holy One of
Israel, thy Saviour . . ."

Tom Sawyer Surveying

The best raft was under way.
"I Go Pogo" had already gone.

Finally the third raft (which was ours) headed out and
away with the current — still afloat. We waved goodbye to those on
shore. They were quickly lost from view as we went through the first
rapid (safely) and around the bend.

This was the final trip of J.C. days.
It had taken two days to build the rafts:

chopped balsa logs floated downstream.
logs lined-up and ridge-poled together.
balsa bark — for tying purposes.
machetes, stone-hammers and LaVera —
      the only tools.

And it was finished!

The staff had suggested its lack of sea-worthiness.
But we would be floating on a river.

The day was with us
                     — as was the current.

Six hours of poling and drifting
                     — toward the airstrip.

Log notations varied
                     — as did observations.

Ahead of us lay

>   the trails to the Mayan Ruins,
>   the final nights in hammocks,
>   the air-flight out
>   home — for some,
>   tribal experience for others
>   (and monkey pressured for breakfast.)

Ahead of us lay

>   the possibility
>   of surveying Bibleless areas
>   for the Gospel's sake;
>   the need for varied transportation
>   and keen observations;
>   (and the Word translated for them.)

BUT FOR THEN —

>   We were modern Tom Sawyers
>   surrounded by God's creation
>   in all of its beauty.
>   We knew the restfulness
>   of drifting down the river.

For those six hours —

>   Our cares were few.
>   Our joys many.

We listened

>   to the happy chatter,
>   the splash of the swimmers,
>   the hymns on the harmonica,
>   the hum of the motor boat passing by.

Ahead of us lay

> future surveying,
> the searching out of lands
> for Bibleless tribes.

BUT FOR THEN —

> We were at peace with God . . .
> in those restful, drifting hours
> our hearts were searched out
> our ways surveyed.

"Search (us), *O God, and know* (our) *hearts; try* (us) *and know* (our) *thoughts:*

And see if there by any wicked way in (us), *and lead* (us) *in the way everlasting."*

Looking Ahead

THE FUTURE!

this training is almost over.
this jungle camp of God's appointment for
these past weeks will soon end.

We trust that we go a bit wiser
and more like Him!

THE FUTURE!

Some will be here for other sessions
— to lead and train new campers.
Some will spread out through Mexico
— with the Gospel of Good News.
Others will go further —
to Vietnam,
Alaska,
Brazil,
the Philippines.
(and some day Africa, Siberia . . .)

For each is called — and each will be guided
in a different direction.

THE FUTURE!

We will be found in many capacities.
Some will be pulled from leadership and tribes
to serve as J.C. staff.
Some will spend their years in translating
this Gospel of Good News.

Others will fly — or build — or teach —
or tend the sick.

(each with a united purpose.)

For each is purposed — that the Bibleless tribes shall hear.

Already some have dropped out along the way

> in poor health.
> by temporary delay.
> for new assignments.
> for unexpected ones.

Endless goodbyes.
> Endless changes.

THE FUTURE!

> surely His coming draweth nigh.
> this time for gathering in the Harvest will soon end.

> AND WE SHALL APPEAR BEFORE HIM —
> AND BE LIKE HIM!

> "with some from every tribe and tongue."

And as we go — some will drop out along the way

> in poor health.
> by temporary delay.
> for new assignments.
> for unexpected ones
> . . . in death.

AND THESE? *". . . the dead in Christ shall rise first. Then we which are alive and remain shall be caught up together with them in the clouds, to meet the Lord in the air: and so shall we ever be with the Lord."*

OH ENDLESS LIFE!

> *"Beloved,*

> *now are we the sons of God, and it doth not yet appear what we shall be, but we know that when He shall appear,*
> > *WE SHALL BE LIKE HIM:*

> > *for we shall see HIM AS HE IS."*

The Imaginary Line

"Behold, how good and how pleasant it is for brethren to dwell together in unity."

It was only a hasty goodbye glimpse of the campers as the M.A.F. plane lifted skyward — the first flight out from Advance Base.

A passenger was delivered.
A mail-meat drop was accomplished (successfully).
An hour's flight-time was ended.
Then our pilot bounced onto another air-strip and deposited Jinnie Lou and me.

Placing our duffles beside us, the pilot was
off and up again.

A browned, perspiring missionary acknowledged
us briefly.

His young son gave a similar nod.

The Indians certainly noticed us
(as though we were curios).

We waited in the hot blistering sun
without eye shade
or helmets
without chairs,
with worn patience.

The motor was finally running.

We were taken by motor-boat across the river to the missionary's home.

Vi was there —

> a friend from the summer school days
> and now "to-be" our senior missionary
> (because of her partner's invitation).

Four Chol believers were there (from our village).

> also the missionary's wife
> and his daughter
> and a barking dog.

Vi found helmets for us —

> changed,
> and then hustled us into the waiting canoe.
> The four believers were to pole us to the village.

The sun beat down warmer.

> We lost one hat
> — the price of a prank.
> And a hanky.

We turned back

> several canoe lengths
> but never caught the hat.
> Nor the hanky.

They poled on —

> Smiles and laughter.
> Shiny, white teeth.
> Bare feet. Browned bodies.

Another hat went overboard —

> (another loss).
> More laughter. More teasing.
> More Chol — the language of these people.

Five and a half hours up the river.
Another hour over the trail
　　　　(and over the burned milpas.)

Then! We saw it.

　　The lovely village of Zapote
　　　　With thatched-roof huts
　　　　　　Set against a background
　　　　　　　　Of mountains and sky and greenery.

Then! They came.

　　The lovely village people
　　　　To welcome the three school teachers — and to stare.
　　　　The scrawny dogs barked and followed.

This was to be the greatest learning ground.
　　Here we would meet the greatest challenges.
　　　　This would be the place of tears and triumphs.

　　　　　(FOR EVER SO BRIEF A TIME.)

　　These Chols of Zapote would show a wonderful
　　simplicity of faith.
　　Here we would know no imaginary line!

　　　　　(THANK GOD FOR THIS!)

The Lord dealt with our hearts.
　— more specifically with mine —
　　　　regarding Himself
　　　　　and others
　　　　　　and missionary service.

We began to learn in those few short weeks that it was right for them to come into our two-roomed thatched home for actually it was theirs, but loaned to us. We began to learn that they had rights which we did not possess because this was their land, their village, their home. And, thank God! — they came (on every waking hour). In their coming we knew acceptance.

Could we who owned nothing outside of Christ resent them for coming? for touching our things? for touching us? for watching us? for peering through the cracks in the house? Thank God! for Vi who loved them for themselves and for their coming. How grateful we were that the Lord dealt with our own hearts concerning this! Thank God! — there was no imaginary line.

How eagerly they came to read (and how often). What class room could thrill three teachers more than one with men and boys or women and children wanting to learn? Discipline was never a problem more than a giggle or two or a shy reader. To hear them read — suddenly with understanding was thrilling. But to hear them read God's Word in their own language with understanding was to cause us truly to rejoice. We were challenged by them in their eagerness.

But more!

We were challenged by them in their simplicity of faith. How they loved Him, those who knew Him, and how they yearned to please Him. They had never sung in their godless days — but now they sang with joy and with reverence. And those who knew Him not called those who believed — SINGERS. Thank God! — for those who SING!

"And what does God's Word say? . . . Then we will do it."

They knew how to worship Him collectively and individually and in their homes. And we who had gone to minister to them found them ministering to us.

Nicolas and Manuel. My little friends! Such great expectations flashed through my mind concerning them. To take them and to transplant them back home. To dress them and to teach them in a culture that I knew. What fun that would be. And what potential.

And the Lord dealt with our hearts
   — and more specifically with mine.

No missionary is sent to another land to transplant people. No missionary goes to introduce his own culture. Nor does a new American or Canadian suit change them. God sends that these might know His Son and that in knowing Him lives might be transformed.

There was still that sad memory of an imaginary line
    of another missionary and his home.
       It seemed somehow to separate
          him from the people
             to whom he had gone.

    (He lived in his own home behind the gate
    "Holding forth the Word of life . . . " but
    withholding his own hand and himself.)

Thank God on reflecting on Zapote and the Chols, one finds that God is concerned that there be no boundary line, that we love them for themselves all the while we are loving them for His own dear Name's sake.

Only as we know Him can imaginary lines be erased.

Only as we know Him better can we live as those "allowed of God to be put in trust with the Gospel . . . " Help us speak, dear Lord, "not as pleasing men, but God, which trieth our hearts."

May we so live that we can say with Paul that we "*. . . being affectionately desirous of* (them) *. . . were willing to have imparted unto* (them), *not the Gospel of God only, but also our own souls, because* (they) *were dear unto us.*"

His Appointed Place

"O taste and see that the Lord is good: blessed is the man that trusteth in Him."

"O taste and see . . . "

I have tasted!
I have seen!

It was more than a glance and more than words when he spoke of returning. His heart was south of the border. His preparations were geared toward it! He had tasted — and seen — life on foreign soil for the Gospel's sake. And he wanted to go back.

The short epistle from Oregon, the hastily written letter from Canada, the frequent messages from North Dakota and Norman all offer similar content. There is a longing to go back. There is that sudden, fresh awareness that they are counted as "chosen vessels" and the fear, "Why me? — weak, foolish, inefficient?" — when all of the time that is why He chose them.

They expressed an almost distaste for the busy-ness of city living and a yearning to be about the "Father's business." They had tasted and they had seen that the Lord was good. They had tasted and seen life in Christ and Christ in lives on foreign soil. And it was good.

There is that wait for an assignment. In time one finds that it is not an ultimate maximum. Nothing and no one can be set as a goal. Nor can time. Only Christ.

The assignment comes
and brings
            numerous minute details,
            unexpected complexities
            and further preparation.

For some —
    the field is always known.
    God has led in that way.

For others —
    the Board must choose
    or circumstances must lead
    or love will afford influence.

In all cases —
    His appointed place is desired!

BUT —
    when all of the props are taken
    and all of the personal desires
        lay crumbled at the feet
      the country itself is not important
      the specific assignment is but a name.
      not even the call is important:

      THE ISSUE IS OBEDIENCE.

The end results must be peace and joy!

God's call
      is not necessarily to a country
           nor tribe
           nor people
           but a call to HIMSELF!

      And He will be manifested.
      And He will be glorified.
      And we will be able to say, *"Now thanks be unto God,*
which always causeth us to triumph in Christ, and maketh manifest
the savour of His knowledge by us IN EVERY PLACE."

His appointed place is His place for us.
The greatest appointment is eternal.

"Let not your heart be troubled: ye believe in God, believe also in me. In my Father's house are many mansions: if it were not so, I would have told you. I go to prepare a place for you. And if I go and prepare a place for you, I will come again, and receive you unto myself; that where I am, there ye may be also.

Then shall we know Him as we are known.
Then shall we be like Him.
Then shall we see Him as He is.
Then shall we joy in His appointed place.

We have tasted.
Some day we shall SEE . . .

And Those at Home

In a sense the place where God sends us is home.
Yet in another sense home will ever be where mom
    and dad and those we love are.

        A motel room can be home.
        A thatched-roof, mud hut can be home.
        A lean-to champa can be home.
        A hammock swaying in a jungle can be home.

It is hard for our families and friends to understand this
(and to accept it).

It is far easier for us to leave
        than for them to remain.
Yet they share in this ministry with us.

        It is good to be remembered and loved.
        It is richer to be upheld in prayer.
        It is ever an encouragement to be sent by them.

And do you (whom we leave behind) share with us?

Are not those whom we are privileged to lead to
Christ, your trophies of grace as well?

Are you not praying for them (and for us)?

Will we not reap the same reward?

AND THEY SAID, "*. . . BECAUSE they went not with us,
we will not give them ought of the spoil
that we have recovered . . . "*

THEN SAID DAVID, *"YE shall not do so, my brethren,
with that which the Lord hath given
us . . . but as his part is that goeth
down to the battle, so shall his part
be that tarrieth by the stuff:*

THEY SHALL PART ALIKE.

AND IT WAS SO."

Epilogue

A Final Happening

The Climb and the Climber

On the eighth anniversary
of life's greatest spiritual defeat
      the Climber
      faced her mountain again.
      Crying out as Caleb had done
      "Lord, give me this mountain."
           Let me climb El Capulin.

My Anakims are still there.

        The towering trees of the jungle
        with arm-like branches
        tearing
        scratching
        trapping
        delaying

          any climb and any climber.

        The towering trees with twisted roots,
        some hidden from sight,
        clutching
        grabbing
        tripping
        hindering

          every climb and every climber.

The sounds of the jungle are still there
awakening fears.

      whispering, whistling winds in the tree tops.
      snapping, crackling twigs beneath the feet.
      clapping, roaring thunder — pattering rain.
      rippling, bubbling sounds of a mountain stream.
      the animal cries — shrieking, chirping songs.
      the rustling, stirring snake in the leaves
      and the weary, panting breathing

          of any climb, any climber.

My Anakims are still there.

      The shame of that first struggling climb:
      crushed
      bruised
      beaten
      defeated
         rocked from deep roots.

      The pride — the cocky sway — proud heart:
      quivering
      tottering
      lurching
      reeling
         no longer sure.

      The dreams and goals before the climb
      (afterward)
      crumbled
      shattered
      decayed
      destroyed
         as dust at her feet.

And the shoes — reminding her of failure
(and selfishness)
burned
ripped
useless
painfully
    pressed upon her feet
    AND THE HEART
    of this climb and this climber.

These were her Anakims.
These lay on those mountain slopes.
These waited hauntingly there
jabbing at memory
    like a range of mountains
    pointed
    rugged
    distant
    yet luring.

Like Caleb, the Climber's
cities are still great and fenced.

    Two villages set on high
    in isolation, far away.

    the Lacandons, totally rejecting Christ.
    the Tzeltals, struggling —
        like the Church of Ephesus —
        to regain its first love.

Great villages.
High on a mountain top.

    one totally darkened by Satan's hold.
    one having tasted the greatness of Christ's love.

Fenced villages
high above the foothills.

    one hedged by heartfelt longing for fruit.
    one hedged by prayer for continued growth.

Villages set on a hill
(a mountain hill).

    the Lacandon village edged by civilization
    but controlled by its god-pots and its god-houses,
    clothed in an ancient culture.

    the Tzeltal village edged by civilization
    but controlled in simplicity by a God of love,
    clothed in garments of praise.

These were the climber's cities — great and fenced.
These sat on the top of her mountain.
These challenged her.
These, *with her Anakims*, awaited conquering
        at the end of the climb.
This was the mountain she wanted to climb again.

AND LIKE CALEB:

    "as her strength was *then*, even so is her strength *now*."

BUT UNLIKE CALEB:

    it was not a strong strength
    but human, limited.

On the eighth anniversary
of life's greatest spiritual defeat
    the Climber
    wanted to go back
    and possess the land.

    to bury the memory
    to prove the Lord
    to drive out the fear.

        of the Anakims there.
        The fear — the utter fear —
        of having failed.

        The fear — the gripping fear —
        of having rushed ahead of God's timing.

    And to be able to cry
    from that mountain top,
    in praise to the Lord,
    "Lord, you have given this mountain."

The Climber had known
that one day she would climb again
and thus she borrowed Caleb's prayer:

        "Now, therefore, Lord, give me this mountain."
        For this time she knew
        (as Caleb knew)
        the Lord would be with her
        to drive out the Anakims,
        to conquer the fears,
        to climb the mountain.

Thus once again, "Out through the camp gate she trudged."
    With another crooked line of eager trainees.
    And just over the hillside, the clouds came
    and the drops began to fall.

    BUT

    This time it was not unknown.
    This time boots braced her ankles.
    This time His love encircled her heart.
    This time her eyes saw more than the mud-caked
        heels of the climbers ahead.

    She saw the Lord
    high and lifted up.
    Gently leading.
       Gently loving.
          Gently meeting
            every need.

    And her feet were as "hind's feet in high places."
    And as the hart panting after the water brooks,
    So her heart panted, thirsting after God.

When the climb seemed straight up — and the heat intensive —
When her footing slipped from the broken rocks . . .
When she fell from her hammock into biting red ants . . .
When mud caked her clothes, her arms, her legs . . .
When a fellow climber tugged at her arm
and pulled her from thickened
                slippery
                sliding
                mud . . .
When she stubbed her toe on fallen rocks and hidden twigs . . .
When she rode the mule hour after hour . . .
Fellow climbers saw only
    the weary side
    the limited endurance
    the human weakness.

    THEY DID NOT SEE OR HEAR THE SINGING HEART.

The Climber's Anakims had been driven out
and her giants — her fears — were as little men.

There was beauty in the towering trees
                    the moss
                    the flowers.

There were lessons in the clutching
                        grabbing
                        twisted roots.

There was music in the whispering
                    whistling
                    crackling
                    rippling
                    bubbling
                    sounds of the jungle.

And the shame of that first struggling climb —
the proud cocky sway,
the shattered dreams,
the torn saddle shoes,
the hurt,
the pressing hurt
    were gone!
    COMPLETELY GONE!!!

For God in loving tenderness
had taken them
(as with the climber's sins)
and buried them
as it were in the sea of His forgetfulness
    — in the mud on the mountain slopes.

He spoke gently to the Climber with these words:

"I, even I, am He that blotteth out thy transgressions
for mine own sake
and will not remember thy sins." — nor thy failures —
anymore.

"Yea, I have loved thee with an everlasting love,
therefore,
with loving kindness have I drawn thee."

"Take heart.
Look up.
Keep climbing.
I have given you your mountain."

AND THE CLIMBER JOYED IN HER CLIMB.

SCRIPTURE REFERENCES

GLOSSARY

AGUA ESCONDIDA

An ancient Mayan temple located in the jungles of southern Mexico.

BAER

Phil and Mary Baer are members of Wycliffe Bible Translators, working among the Lacandon Indians, located a one day hike from Jungle Camp.

CHAMPA

A rustic, temporary shelter built from jungle materials.

CHOL

An Indian language group located north and west of Jungle Camp.

EL CAPULIN

A small native settlement where coffee is grown. Jungle Camp trainees often spend the night here on their trip to visit the Lacandon Indians.

IXTAPA

A small town near a main highway where the Missionary Aviation (MAF) airplane serving Jungle Camp was based before relocating in San Cristobal de Las Casas.

LACANDONS

A small language group of Mayan Indians, thought by many to be remnants of the ancient Mayan priests.

MILPAS

An Indian corn field filled with tree stumps.

MORRALES

A flat carrying bag with a long strap to go over the shoulder or over the forehead.

TZELTAL

The Indian language group in the Jungle Camp area.

YAXOQUINTELA

The Tzeltal name for Jungle Camp Main Base. It is named for a stream close by, the meaning of the word being "running green water."

ZAPOTE

The name given to a CHOL Indian village.

Pacific Ocean

Mexico

Gulf of Mexico

Guatemala

Legend

	River Canyon	●	Farms and Ranches
	Air field	●	Towns
	Trails		

Kilometers

1: 250 000

0   5   10   15   20

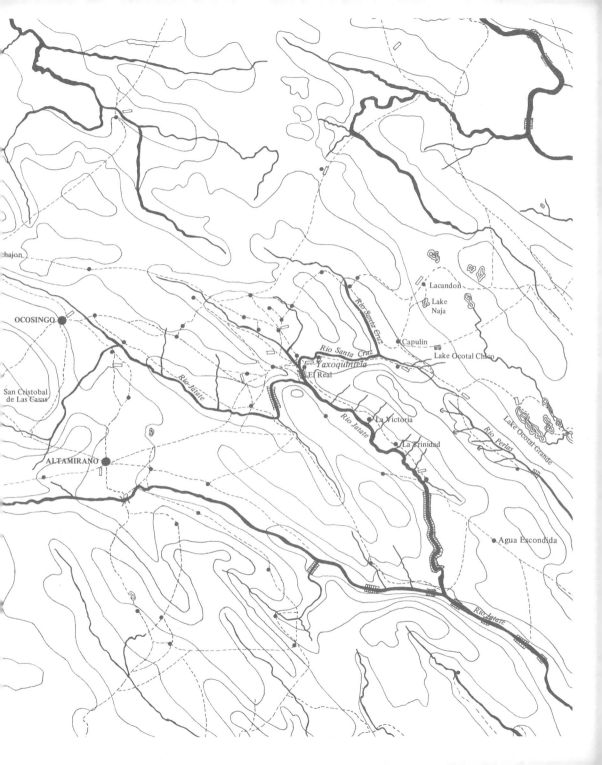